TONY HOAGLAND

UNINCORPORATED PERSONS IN THE PERSONS IN THE LATE HONDA DYNASTY

BLOODAXE BOOKS

ISBN: 978 1 85224 872 7

This edition published 2010 by
Bloodaxe Books Ltd,
Highgreen,
Tarset,
Northumberland NE48 1RP.

First published in the USA
by Graywolf Press in 2010.

www.bloodaxebooks.com
For further information about Bloodaxe titles
please visit our website or write to
the above address for a catalogue.

Supported by
ARTS COUNCIL
ENGLAND

Typesetting: BookMobile Design and Publishing Services, Minneapolis, MN.
Book design: Rachel Holscher.
Cover design: Neil Astley & Pamela Robertson-Pearce.

Printed in Great Britain by
Bell & Bain Limited, Glasgow, Scotland.

for Dean Young, the Irreplacable

and for Jason, the Real

Contents

III.

There are words that mean nothing
But there is something to mean.
George Oppen, "The Building of the Skyscraper"

Whatever made sugarcane sweet
Rumi (trans. Coleman Barks)

I.

Description

A bird with a cry like a cell phone says something
to a bird which sounds like a manual typewriter.

Out of sight in the woods, the creek trickles
its ongoing sentence; from treble to baritone,

from dependent clause to interrogative.

The trees rustle over the house: they are excited
to be entering the poem

in late afternoon, when the clouds are creamy and massive,
as if to illustrate contentment.

And maybe a wind will pluck off the last dead leaves;
and a cold rain will splash

dainty white petals from the crab apple tree
down to the ground,

the pink and the brown mingled there,
like two different messages scribbled over each other.

In all of this a place must be
reserved for human suffering:

the sick and unloved, the chemically confused;
the ones who believe desperately in insight;
the ones addicted to change.

How our thoughts clawed and pummeled the walls.
How we tried but could not find our way out.

In the wake of our effort, how we rested.
How description was the sign of our acceptance.

Food Court

If you want to talk about America, why not just mention
Jimmy's Wok and Roll American-Chinese Gourmet Emporium?—
the cloud of steam rising from the bean sprouts and shredded cabbage

when the oil is sprayed on from a giant plastic bottle
wielded by Ramon, Jimmy's main employee,
who hates having to wear the sanitary hair net

and who thinks the food smells funny?
And the secretaries from the law firm
                    drifting in from work at noon
to fill the tables of the food court,
in their cotton skirts and oddly sexy running shoes?

Why not mention the little grove of palm trees
maintained by the mall corporation
and the splashing fountain beside it

and the faint smell of dope-smoke drifting from the men's room
where two boys from the suburbs
dropped off by their moms

with their baggy ghetto pants and skateboards
are getting ready to pronounce their first sentences
                          in African-American?

Oh yes, everything
all chopped up and stirred together
                    in the big steel pan
held over a medium-high blue flame

while Jimmy watches
with his practical black eyes.

Big Grab

The corn-chip engineer gets a bright idea,
and talks to the corn-chip executive
and six months later at the factory they begin subtracting
a few chips from every bag,

but they still call it on the outside wrapper,
The Big Grab,
so the concept of *Big* is quietly modified
to mean *More Or Less Large,* or *Only Slightly*
                                    Less Big Than Before.

Confucius said this would happen—
that language would be hijacked and twisted
by a couple of tricksters from the Business Department

and from then on words would get crookeder and crookeder
until no one would know how to build a staircase,
or to size up a horse by its teeth
or when it is best to shut up.

We live in that time that he predicted.
Nothing means what it says,
and it says it all the time.
Out on Route 28, the lights blaze all night
on a billboard of a beautiful girl
covered with melted cheese—

See how she beckons to the river of late-night cars!
See how the tipsy drivers swerve,
under the breathalyzer moon!

In a story whose beginning I must have missed,
without a name for the thing
I can barely comprehend I desire,

I speak these words that do not know
where they're going.

No wonder I want something more or less large
and salty for lunch.
No wonder I stare into space while eating it.

Romantic Moment

After seeing the nature documentary we walk down Canyon Road,
onto the plaza of art galleries and high end clothing stores

where the orange trees are fragrant in the summer night
and the smooth adobe walls glow fleshlike in the dark.

It is just our second date, and we sit down on a bench,
holding hands, not looking at each other,

and if I were a bull penguin right now I would lean over
and vomit softly into the mouth of my beloved

and if I were a peacock I'd flex my gluteal muscles to
erect and spread the quills of my Cinemax tail.

If she were a female walkingstick bug she might
insert her hypodermic proboscis delicately into my neck

and inject me with a rich hormonal sedative
before attaching her egg sac to my thoracic undercarriage,

and if I were a young chimpanzee I would break off a nearby tree limb
and smash all the windows in the plaza jewelry stores.

And if she was a Brazilian leopard frog she would wrap her impressive
tongue three times around my right thigh and

pummel me lightly against the surface of our pond
and I would know her feelings were sincere.

Instead we sit awhile in silence, until
she remarks that in the relative context of tortoises and iguanas,

human males seem to be actually rather expressive.
And I say that female crocodiles really don't receive

enough credit for their gentleness.
Then she suggests that it is time for us to go

do something personal, hidden, and human.

I Have News for You

There are people who do not see a broken playground swing
as a symbol of ruined childhood

and there are people who don't interpret the behavior
of a fly in a motel room as a mocking representation of their thought process.

There are people who don't walk past an empty swimming pool
and think about past pleasures unrecoverable

and then stand there blocking the sidewalk for other pedestrians.
I have read about a town somewhere in California where human beings

do not send their sinuous feeder roots
deep into the potting soil of others' emotional lives

as if they were greedy six-year-olds
sucking the last half-inch of milkshake up through a noisy straw;

and other persons in the Midwest who can kiss without
debating the imperialist baggage of heterosexuality.

Do you see that creamy, lemon-yellow moon?
There are some people, unlike me and you,

who do not yearn after fame or love or quantities of money as
                    unattainable as that moon;
thus, they do not later
                         have to waste more time
defaming the object of their former ardor.

Or consequently run and crucify themselves
in some solitary midnight Starbucks Golgotha.

I have news for you—
there are people who get up in the morning and cross a room

and open a window to let the sweet breeze in
and let it touch them all over their faces and bodies.

Plastic

One could probably explain the whole world in terms of Plastic: the plastic
used for almost everything—the little ivory forks at picnics
                        and green toy dinosaurs in playrooms everywhere;

the rooks and pawns of cheap $4.95 chess sets made in the People's
    Republic of China

and those Tupperware containers that open with a perfect quiet pop
to yield the tuna fish sandwich
about to enter the mouth of the secretary on his lunch break.

You could talk about how the big molecules were bound in chains
by chemical reactions, then liquefied and poured like soup

into intricate factory molds
for toy soldiers and backscratchers, airsick bags and high-tech Teflon
    roof racks;

you could mull over the ethics of enslaving matter
                        even while feeling admiration for the genius it takes

to persuade a molecule to become part of a casserole container.

And what about plastic that has become dear to you?
Personal plastic?
                —the toothbrush and the flip-flops,

the hollow plastic Easter egg that held jellybeans inside,
the twelve-inch vinyl disk that in 1976 brought you Copacetic Brown and
                the Attorneys of Cool?

Plastic companions into which the lonely heart was poured,
                which gave it color and a shape?

—Or in another case, the blue polyethylene water bottle
sitting on a table in the park on Saturday

between two people having a talk about their relationship

—which I could tell was probably near its end
since the various lubrications
                              usually coating the human voice

were all worn away, leaving just the rough, gritty surfaces
of need and fear
              exposed and rubbing on each other.

I wonder if it would have done any good then
if I had walked over and explained a few things to them

about Plastic?
About how it is so much easier to stretch than
                                    human nature,

which accounts for some of the strain imposed on
                              the late 20th-century self,
occasionally causing what has been called Interpersonal Adhesive
    Malfunction.

They might have been relieved to know
that science has a name
for their feelings at that precise moment of modern living,

which may be why each of them kept reaching out
to seize the plastic water bottle

and suck from it
in fierce little hydraulic gulps,

as if the water was helping them to wash down something hard to ingest;
    or the bottle was a life vest keeping them afloat on open sea—

though their pink elastic lips, wrapped around the stem of the container
were so much more beautiful than plastic

and the smooth ripple
of their flexible muscular throats

made the only sound audible
above the tough, indifferent silence
                    starting to stretch over everything.

Hard Rain

After I heard *It's a Hard Rain's A-Gonna Fall*
played softly by an accordion quartet
through the ceiling speakers at the Springdale Shopping Mall,
I understood: there's nothing
we can't pluck the stinger from,

nothing we can't turn into a soft-drink flavor or a t-shirt.
Even serenity can become something horrible
if you make a commercial about it
using smiling, white-haired people

quoting Thoreau to sell retirement homes
in the Everglades, where the swamp has been
drained and bulldozed into a nineteen-hole golf course
with electrified alligator barriers.

"You can't keep beating yourself up, Billy,"
I heard the therapist say on television
                                     to the teenage murderer,
"about all those people you killed—
You just have to be the best person you can be,
                        one day at a time—"

And everybody in the audience claps and weeps a little,
because the level of deep feeling has been touched,
and they want to believe that
the power of Forgiveness is greater
than the power of Consequence, or History.

Dear Abby:
My father is a businessman who travels.
Each time he returns from one of his trips,
his shoes and trousers
    are covered with blood—
but he never forgets to bring me a nice present.
Should I say something?
                 Signed, America.

I used to think I was not part of this,
that I could mind my own business and get along,

but that was just another song
that had been taught to me since birth—

whose words I was humming under my breath,
as I was walking thorough the Springdale Mall.

Confinement

The dictator in the turban died, and was replaced
by a dictator in a Western business suit.
Now that he looked like all the other leaders, observers

detected a certain relaxing of tensions. Something in the air
said the weather was changing.
and if you looked up at the sky and squinted, you could see

the faint dollar signs embossed on the big, migrating clouds,
sucking up cash in one place, raining it down in another.
Meanwhile I was trying to get across town,

to my brother-in-law's funeral,
speeding through yellow lights, arriving late,
taking my place in a line of idling cars

outside the cemetery. Having to wait with everyone else
because no one had gotten the code number
to punch into the keypad on the automatic gate.

Cold day. The neighborhood, ugly and poor,
like a runny nose,
a reminder of misery in the world

and Barney was dead, big Party-Boy Barney,
famous for his lack of self-control—
now needing an extra-large coffin,

as if he was taking his old friends,
Drinking, Smoking, and Eating
into the hole with him.

Later, at the reception, I saw my beautiful ex-wife,
wearing a simple black dress
that showed off her beautiful neck,

standing next to a man I would like to call
her future second ex-husband.
A long time since she and I had been extinct,

but still I found inside myself a fierce desire
to go over and tell her again that it wasn't my fault—
and struggled for a moment with that ridiculous urge.

Upstairs, looking for a place to be alone,
I found a television, turned on and abandoned in a room,
churning out pictures and light against a wall—

images of crowds, marching down streets, past
burning, overturned cars; people in robes,
gathered outside embassies, and throwing stones.

Even with the sound off,
not even knowing the name of the country,
I thought that I could understand

what they were protesting about,
what had made them so angry:

they wanted to be let out of the TV set;
they had been trapped in there, and they wanted out.

Love

The middle-aged man
who cannot make love to his wife
with the erectile authority of yesteryear
must lower his head and suck her breasts
with the tenderness and acumen of Walt Whitman.

And if the woman has lost her breasts
to the surgeon and his silver knife,
she must hump the man's leg in the dark bedroom
like a rodeo bronco rider.

Let them be hard and wet again, respectively.
Let them convince, and be convinced.

It is the kind of heroic performance
that no one will ever mention.
It is the part of the journey where the staircase gets narrow
and you must turn sideways to pass.

Over the earth the clouds mutate and roll.
The trees catch their breath for another try.
Wind rips through the dried-out grass
                              with a threshing sound.

The man going under the covers.
The woman letting him.
Both of them refusing
to be stopped by shame.

All that talk about love, and *This*
is what that word was pointing at.

"Poor Britney Spears"

is not a sentence I expected
to utter in this lifetime.

If *she* wants to make a career comeback
so her agent gets her a spot on the MTV awards show
but she can't lose the weight beforehand

so looks a little chubby in a spangled bikini
before millions of fanged, spiteful fans and enemies
and gets a little drunk beforehand
so misses a step in the dance routine,

making her look, one critic says,
like a "comatose piglet,"

well, it wasn't by accident, was it?
That she wandered into the late-twentieth-century glitterati party
of striptease American celebrity?

First we made her into an object of desire,
then into an object of contempt,
now we want to turn her into an object of compassion?

Are you sure we know what the hell we're doing?

Is she a kind of voodoo doll
onto whom we project
our vicarious fantasies of triumph and humiliation?

Is she a pink, life-size piece of chewing gum
full of non-FDA approved additives
engineered by the mad scientists
of the mainstream dream machine?

Or is she nothing less than a gladiatrix
who strolls into the coliseum
full of blinding lights and tigers

with naught but her slim javelin of talent
and recklessly little protective clothing?

Oh my adorable little monkey,
prancing for your candy,

with one of my voices I shout, "Jump! Jump, you little whore!"
With another I say,

in a quiet way that turns down the lights,
"Put on some clothes and go home, Sweetheart."

The Story of the Father

This is another story that I sometimes think about:
the story of the father

after the funeral of his son the suicide,
going home and burning all the photographs of that dead boy;

standing next to the backyard barbecue,
feeding the pictures to the fire; watching the pale smoke
rise and disappear into the humid Mississippi sky;

aware that he is standing at the edge of some great border,
ignorant that he is hogging all the pain.

How quiet the suburbs are in the middle of an afternoon
when a man is destroying evidence,
breathing in the chemistry of burning Polaroids,

watching the trees over the rickety fence
seem to lift and nod in recognition.

Later, he will be surprised
by the anger of his family:

the wife hiding her face in her hands,
the daughter calling him names,

—but for now, he is certain of his act; now

he is like a man destroying a religion,
or hacking at the root of a tree.

Over and over I have arrived here just in time
to watch the father use a rusty piece of wire

to nudge the last photo of the boy
into the orange part of the flame:

the face going brown, the memory undeveloping.

It is not the misbegotten logic of the father;
it is not the pity of the snuffed-out youth;

it is the old intelligence of pain
that I admire:

how it moves around inside of him like smoke;

how it knows exactly what to do with human beings
to stay inside of them forever.

The Situation

When the pain was fresh,
for a while the problem got very clear

and the clarity constituted a kind of relief
as if the problem had withdrawn
to watch what you would do.

But after a while the clarity began to fade,
and three days later you couldn't have articulated
precisely what the problem *was*,

and three days after that you forgot
that there even was a problem,
and your old way of thinking resumed.

You're just a citizen
of your own familiarity
who can't remember himself in a different way.

You go along and every now and then
the path jumps out from under you.
And you have learned to expect this upheaval,

as much as that is possible.
One might say it is with a kind of fidelity
that you keep making your mistakes,

and then renewing them,
as if you were following a sign that says,

This Way to Freshness.

Expensive Hotel

When the middle-class black family in the carpeted hall
passes the immigrant housekeeper from Belize, oh
that is an interesting moment. One pair of eyes is lowered.

That's how you know you are part
of a master race—when someone
humbles themselves without even having to be asked.

And in that moment trembling
from the stress of its creation,
we feel the illness underneath our skin—

the unquenchable wish to be thought well of
wilting and dying a little
while trying to squeeze by

the cart piled high with fresh towels and sheets,
small bars of soap and bottles
of bright green shampoo,

which are provided for guests to steal.

Hostess

All I remember from that party
is the little black dress of the hostess
held up by nothing more
than a shoestring of raw silk

that kept slipping off her shoulder
—so the whole time she was talking to you
about real estate or vinaigrette,

you would watch it gradually
slide down her satiny arm
until the very last moment
when she shrugged it back in place again.

Oh the business of that dress
was non-specific and unspeakable,
and it troubled all of us

like the boundary of a disputed territory
or the edge of a borderline personality.
It was like a story you wanted to see
brought to a conclusion, but

it was also like a story stuck
in the middle of itself, as it kept on
almost happening, but not,
then almost happening again—

It took all night for me to understand
the dress was designed to fail like that;
the hostess was designed to keep it up,
as we were designated to chew

the small rectangles of food
they serve at such affairs, and to salivate
while the night moved us around in its mouth.

This is the way in which parties
are dreamlike, duplicitous places
where you hang in a kind of suspense
between the real and the pretended.

All I remember from that night
is that I had come for a mysterious reason,
which I waited to see revealed.

And that, by the end of the evening,
I had found my disappointment,
which I hoped no one else had seen.

Complicit with Everything

The weed that sprouted from the dirt
under the drip-drop-drip of the air-conditioner

fastened itself to the gray drainpipe;
inched up the apartment building wall,

then headed horizontally west on the thin dark cord
stapled to the wall by the cable TV guy—

looping around and around, and leafing out,
like bright green embroidery against white siding,

—past the apartment of the widow with cats
and the retired bachelor mailman Bill,

watcher of sports events and CNN atrocities—
unhappy possessor of cancer in the left lung,

a man who wants to stay in touch
with the whole wide world but doesn't know

that this healthy green cousin is staking its claim
just below his conceptual horizon,

nourished by water from his very own air-conditioner
while decoratively dressing up the exterior

of a building that has seen better days
—this green, persistent vegetable

that doesn't seem to mind the taste of secondhand moisture
or the bloodthirsty roar of the crowd

as a quarterback is fed to the defensive line,
and they thrive in a kind of greedy innocence,

the vine and the mailman
and the cancer and the air-conditioner,

complicit with nothing but everything.

II.

At the Galleria

Just past the bin of pastel baby socks and underwear,
there are some 49-dollar Chinese-made TVs;

one of them singing news about a far-off war,
one comparing the breast size of an actress

from Hollywood to the breast size
of an actress from Bollywood.

And here is my niece Lucinda,
who is nine and a daughter of Texas,

who has developed the flounce of a pedigreed blonde
and declares that her favorite sport is shopping.

Today is the day she embarks upon her journey,
swinging a credit card like a scythe

through the meadows of golden merchandise.
Today is the day she stops looking at faces,

and starts assessing the price of purses;
So let it begin. Let her be dipped in the dazzling bounty

and raised and wrung out again and again.
And let us watch.

As the gods in olden stories
turned mortals into laurel trees and crows
                        to teach them some kind of lesson,

so we were turned into Americans
to learn something about loneliness.

Address to the Beloved

Sweetie,
what do you mean
when you tell me to get real?

Do you mean that I should stop
slipping my hand down the back of your pants
when we are out in public?

Or that I should do it more often?
Do you mean I should acquaint myself better
with Baltic-state politics?

Or scrape and wash the dishes in the sink
right after we have eaten?
Should I stop trying to flirt

with the whole wide world,
and get down to business,
or the reverse?
Get more health insurance, water the lawn,
read philosophy at night?

When you say "real," are you implying
I need to fire the shrink,
become more austere,
less sentimental about my friends?

Or do you mean that I should simply
stand here,
without being clever or cute,
enduring the light

when what I want is to
hide my face
or to crawl inside you like a cupboard
and live on your feelings

instead of my own?

When you say I leave a lot to be desired,
is that a good thing?

When you said you would leave me
to my own devices,

what did you mean? Did you mean this?

Cement Truck

I wanted to get the cement truck into the poem
because I loved the bulk of the big rotating barrel
    as it went calmly down the street,
churning to keep the wet cement inside
            slushily in motion.

I liked the monster girth of the torso
      and the tilted ovoid shape,
the raised rump with a hole like an anus at the back,
the double-thick tires to bear the weight. I liked
    the way that people turned to watch it pass—

because what is more like a rhinoceros or elephant
than this thick-skinned grunting beast
    goaded by two smallish men in jumpsuits?
Taking its ponderous time to obey,
     drizzling a stream of juice between its legs?

I knew that I might have to make the center of the poem wider
when the cement truck had to turn a corner,
     scraping the bark of an overhanging tree,
giving a nudge to the power lines—

then having to turn around again, because
the drivers have somehow gotten lost:
one of them running to borrow a garden hose
        to wet down the load again,
one of them cursing and shaking out the map.

I liked the idea of my poem having room inside
for something as real as that truck
and having to get there by two o'clock or else
to pour the floor of the high-school gymnasium.

—And I think at this point it would have been a terrible mistake
to turn the truck
into a metaphor or symbol for something else.
It had taken me so long to get the world into my poem,
and so long to get my poem into the world.

Now I didn't want to go back.
Now I had a four-lane highway to drive down the middle of,
and a pair of heavy rubber boots,
and a black rectangular lever just in front of the stick shift.

I wonder what that one does?

In Praise of Their Divorce

And when I heard about the divorce of my friends,
I couldn't help but be proud of them,

that man and that woman setting off in different directions,
like pilgrims in a proverb

—him to buy his very own toaster oven,
her seeking a prescription for sleeping pills.

Let us keep in mind the hidden forces
which had struggled underground for years

to push their way to the surface—and that finally did,
cracking the crust, moving the plates of earth apart,

releasing the pent-up energy required
for them to rent their own apartments,

for her to join the softball league for single mothers
for him to read *George the Giraffe* over his speakerphone

at bedtime to the six-year-old.

The bible says, *Be fruitful and multiply*

but is it not also fruitful to subtract and to divide?
Because if marriage is a kind of womb,

divorce is the being born again;
alimony is the placenta one of them will eat;

loneliness is the name of the wet-nurse;
regret is the elementary school;

endurance is the graduation.
So do not say that they are splattered like dropped lasagna

or dead in the head-on collision of clichés
or nailed on the cross of their competing narratives.

What is taken apart is not utterly demolished.
It is like a great mysterious egg in Kansas

that has cracked and hatched two big bewildered birds.
It is two spaceships coming out of retirement,

flying away from their dead world,
the burning booster rocket of divorce
                              falling off behind them,

the bystanders pointing at the sky and saying, *Look.*

The Loneliest Job in the World

As soon as you begin to ask the question, *Who loves me?*,
you are completely screwed, because
the next question is *How Much?*,

and then it is hundreds of hours later,
and you are still hunched over
your flowcharts and abacus,

trying to decide if you have gotten enough.
This is the loneliest job in the world:
to be an accountant of the heart.

It is late at night. You are by yourself,
and all around you, you can hear
the sounds of people moving

in and out of love,
pushing the turnstiles, putting
their coins in the slots,

paying the price which is asked,
which constantly changes.
No one knows why.

Dialectical Materialism

I was thinking about dialectical materialism at the supermarket,

strolling among the Chilean tomatoes and the Filipino pineapples,

admiring the Washington-state apples stacked in perfect pyramid displays
by the ebony man from Zimbabwe wearing the Chicago Bulls t-shirt.

I was seeing the whole produce section
                    as a system of cross-referenced signifiers
in a textbook of historical economics

and the fine spray that misted the vegetables
was like the cool mist of style imposed on meaning.

It was one of those days
when interpretation is brushing its varnish over everything

when even the birds are speaking complete sentences

and the sun is a brassy blond novelist of immense accomplishment
      dictating her new blockbuster
to a stenographer who types at the speed of light
and publishes each page as fast as it is written.

There was cornbread rising in the bakery department
and in its warm aroma I believed that I could smell
                    the exhaled breath of vanished Iroquois,
their journey west and
                    delicate withdrawal into the forests,

whereas by comparison
the coarse-grained wheat baguettes

seemed to irrepressibly exude
    the sturdy sweat and labor of eighteenth-century Europe.

My god there is so much sorrow in the grocery store!
You would have to be high
on the fumes of the piped-in pan flutes
        of commodified Peruvian folk music

not to be driven practically crazy
with awe and shame,
not to weep at the scale of subjugated matter:

the ripped-up etymologies of kiwi fruit and bratwurst,
the roads paved with dead languages,
the jungles digested by foreign money.

It's the owners, I said to myself;
it's the horrible juggernaut of progress;

but the cilantro in my hand
opened up its bitter minty ampoule underneath my nose

and the bossa nova muzak charmed me like a hypnotist
and the pretty cashier with the shaved head and nose ring
            said, *Have a nice day,*

as I burst with my groceries through the automatic doors
into the open air,

where I found myself in a giant parking lot
at a mega-mall outside of Minneapolis,

where in row E 87
a Ford Escort from Mankato
      had just had a fender-bender with a Honda from Miami;

and these personified portions of my heart, the drivers,
were standing there
in the gathering midwestern granular descending dusk

waiting for the trooper to fill out the accident report,

with the rotating red light of the squad car
                  whipping in circles above them,
splashing their shopped-out middle-aged faces
                  with war paint the hue of cherry Gatorade

and each of them was thinking
how with dialectical materialism, accidents happen:

how at any minute,
convenience can turn
            into a kind of trouble you never wanted.

My Father's Vocabulary

In the history of American speech,
he was born between "Dirty Commies" and "Nice tits."

He worked for Uncle Sam,
and married a dizzy gal from Pittsburgh with a mouth on her.

I was conceived in the decade
between "Far out" and "Whatever";

at the precise moment when "going all the way"
turned into "getting it on."

Sometimes, I swear, I can feel the idiom flying around inside my head
like moths left over from the Age of Aquarius.

Or I hear myself speak and it feels like I am wearing
a no-longer-groovy cologne from the seventies.

In those days I was always trying to get a rap session going,
and he was always telling me how to clean out the garage.

Our last visit took place in the twilight zone of a clinic,
between "feeling no pain" and "catching a buzz."

For that occasion I had carefully prepared
a suitcase full of small talk

—But he was already packed and going backwards,
with the nice tits and the dirty commies,

to the small town of his vocabulary,
somewhere outside of Pittsburgh.

Hinge

Last night on TV the light-brown African-American professor
looked at the printout analysis of his own DNA
and learned that he was mostly Irish.

I can't go back to Africa now, he thought,
controlling the expression on his face,
his big moment onscreen already turning out
different than he had imagined.

Nor would he ever be able to say the sentence,
"I be at the crib"
with the same brotherly ease as before.

I was tired from work, and I wanted to
turn off the television and go to bed,
but I couldn't stop watching that transformation,

the bones in his face rearranging,
his freckles becoming explicable

thanks to the hinge on an 18th-century door
between the kitchen of a Massachusetts merchant
and the southernmost room where a slave-woman slept;

thanks to the macramé of chromosomes, and the electron microscope
and the longing for knowledge
which sometimes makes things more
confusing than they were before.

That's how I feel while I watch, as if
eavesdropping on the family next door,—
pressing my ear to the wall,

slowly starting to make out the words,
not certain why I am so interested.
My ear glued to the wall.

The merchant raising a tiny oilcan, and tilting it
to squeeze three drops
into the hinge to keep it quiet.

Foghorn

When that man my age
came towards me in the fast-food restaurant
with his blue plastic cafeteria tray

and stood next to the table where I sat alone
(there was no place else to sit),
I looked up at him in welcome—

But when a black man and a white man
turn their glances on each other,
the air suddenly fills up with secret signs,

like MLK and NBA, like KKK
and NRA, like DWB and NWA
—and it gets hard to see through
all that smoke and burning shrubbery.

And what with the internal sirens
and the historical foghorn
and the sprinkler system
designed to suppress non-categorical
fraternization

and the voice that says *Impossible*
and the other one that says *Lying Motherfucker*,
you just want to put your hands over your head
and step away from the vehicle.

Here is what we know:
history is a car wreck from which
our parents did not escape;
our nation is a career criminal;
we were raised to be liars and deniers.

Now here we are in time for our own moment
of unequal opportunity,
which we will probably fail to understand
or raise our best selves to.

In this land where consciousness is a fiction,
through the oxygen mask of my lies
and the skin of my self-deception,
this is what I say:

Brother, lean your brown face down
and let me look at you.

The Story of White People

After so long seeming right, as in
true, as in clean, as in smart,
being smart enough at least
not to be born some other color,

after so long being visitors
from the galaxy Caucasia,
now they are starting to seem a little

deficient, leached out, spent, colorless,
thin-blooded, indefinite—
as in being too far and too long
removed from the original source
of whiteness,

suffering from a slight amnesia
in the way that skim milk can barely
remember the cow

and this change in status is
mysterious, indifferent, and objective,
as at the beginning of winter
when the light shifts its angle of attention

from the mulberry to the cottonwood.
Just another change of season,
not that dramatic or perceptible,

but to all of us, it feels a little different.

Personal

Don't take it personal, they said;
but I did, I took it all quite personal—

the breeze and the river and the color of the fields;
the price of grapefruit and stamps,

the wet hair of women in the rain—
and I cursed what hurt me

and I praised what gave me joy,
the most simple-minded of possible responses.

The government reminded me of my father,
with its deafness and its laws,

and the weather reminded me of my mom,
with her tropical squalls.

Enjoy it while you can, they said of Happiness.
Think first, they said of Talk.

Get over it, they said
at the School of Broken Hearts.

But I couldn't and I didn't and I don't
believe in the clean break;

I believe in the compound fracture
served with a sauce of dirty regret;

I believe in saying it all
and taking it all back

and saying it again for good measure,
while the air fills up with *I'm-Sorries*

like wheeling birds
and the trees look seasick in the wind.

Oh life! Can you blame me
for making a scene?

You were that limousine, the moon,
climbing an onramp of pearl gray cloud.

I was the dog, chained in some fool's backyard:
barking and barking,

trying to convince everything else to wake up
and take it personal too.

Jason the Real

If I was a real guy,
said my friend Jason,
and I got an email like that,
what would you *do?*

Someone had told him he was a big sexy dreamboat
and he was trying to figure out
if he should buy a sports car and a condom

or take an Alka-Seltzer and go to bed
to recover from the agitation.

You remember what that was like, don't you?
to be excited by an unexpected pleasure
that is almost immediately turned into a problem?

My friend Jason, gentle guy
with the blood galloping around inside his head
like a wild pony,

changing his shirt thirteen times,
doing the victory dance of the eligible bachelor,
combing his hair and falling over furniture.

That girl had knocked him out of focus
with her sweet words
about finding him pretty

and now he was standing on the Continental Divide,
i.e., whether to remain continent or not—
but he didn't like having to decide.

It is so human to turn a freedom into pain
and it is so sweet when life
comes to teach you suffering

by giving you a choice,
and you twist and turn
in the little flames of possibility.

—But that is how you build your castle.
That is how one earns a name
like Jason the Real.

Visitation

Now when I visit Ellen's body in my memory,
it is like visiting a cemetery. I look
at the chiseled, muscular belly
and at the perfect thirty-year-old breasts
and the fine blonde purse of her pussy
and I kneel and weep a little there.
I am not the first person to locate god
in erectile tissue and the lubricating gland
but when I kiss her breast and feel
the tough button of the nipple
rise and stiffen to my tongue
like the dome of a small mosque
in an ancient, politically-incorrect city,
I feel holy, I begin to understand religion.
I circle around to see the basilica
of her high, Irish-American butt,
and I look at her demure little asshole
and am sorry I didn't spend more time with it.
And her mouth and her eyes and white white teeth.
It's beauty beauty beauty which in a way Ellen
herself the person distracted me from. It's
beauty that has been redistributed now
by the justice of chance and the temporal economy.
Now I'm like a sad astronaut living
deep in space, breathing the oxygen of memory
out of a silver can. Now I'm like an angel
drifting over the surface of the earth,
brushing its meadows and forests
with the tips of my wings,
with wonder and regret and affection.

Rhythm and Blues

And five months later
the snow on the far side of the street had melted,
                    the season changing again and

I was still thinking of my friend Rolf Jordahl
and how strange it was to be sitting in his backyard
                    after his funeral last year,

watching the vines stir softly on the trellis
while his sister and her friends got drunk
                    in clusters on the patio—

I saw the empty dog-food bowl
            someone had taken the trouble to wash out,
            the red plastic O like an open mouth,

and in the bedroom, the shirts piled up on his bed
            for people to go through—

I tell you, it was pretty unpleasant
to watch all of his possessions
            giving up his fingerprints like that—

as someone put on one of his records
      and Etta James began to sing, *I hate to
            see that evening sun go down,*

inside her voice the little bloody sun
      going down in the kitchen window of each syllable,

as I thought to myself Yes, this is what it comes to—
      always a sad woman standing at a sink
            scraping the old food from the plates—

But it will never be alright with me, this moving on,
            the way people let themselves
                        get away with it,

as if life was a series of hotel rooms
                        we leave behind
for someone else to clean,

and memory a little glass of wine
you sip for pleasure and then put down.

I watched the people at that party
            like a policeman taking notes,
sorting out the real tears from the sentimental ones,

noticing the exact moment when
grief smeared into self-pity
            and the ones with unhappy marriages
                        started looking around—

I guess judgment was my way of remembering my friend;
I guess I thought I was defending him
            from being forgotten,

holding on with one hand and
goddamning everybody else
            for not holding on tighter,

but I finally couldn't sort it out

and even my self-righteousness began to wane and lose its torchlike force,

as the sky above the yard grew dim,
            and people moved indoors.

By that time I had one of Rolf's shirts under my arm,
            and was talking to the sister from Minneapolis,

looking at a roomful of faces
            flushed with the effort of forgetting.

This has been the year I will remember
            as the one in which I wore Rolf's shirt,

like a secret and a pledge;
like a penance and critique;
like a fashion statement and an antique.

Each time I put it on, I felt my arm push through
one of the holes he left,

and sometimes, I was surprised not to find him there ahead of me;
and sometimes I just forgot whose shirt it was

—taking the sleeve between my forefinger and thumb,
and rubbing it absent-mindedly,

or sometimes slipping my hand between the buttons
to touch myself.

Summer

God moves mysterious thunderheads over the towns and office buildings,
cracks them open like raw eggs. The north has critical humidity.
The south plucks at its sweaty clothes. The weatherman says it's August,
and a sniper is haunting Washington DC.

He's picking victims at random from shopping malls and parking lots,
touching them with bullets like blue fingertips,

and some say he's an unemployed geek with a chip on his shoulder,
and some say he's an agent of ancient Greek theology.

Gibb says the sniper is a surrealist travel agent
                    booking departures only
Or he's a dada lawyer without a client
                    arguing in thirty-caliber sentences.

Robin says the sniper is what the country invented
                    as a symptom of its mental illness
and Marcia is sad because she knows the sniper could have been cured
by a regimen of vitamins and serotonin reuptake inhibitors.

We had fallen into one of our periodic comas
                    of obesity and celebrity
when the sniper went off like an alarm clock

and the preacher on TV
said that he had come according to Revelation 3:14
to punish us for the crime of not being ready for death—

but as Snoopy the clerk at the 7-11 said,
What kind of crime is that?

Meanwhile the air-conditioners are working overtime,
the rooftops are full of SWAT teams and camera crews
and the sky too is mobilizing:
dark clouds without speaking, menacing millennial clouds.

We don't know yet what the metaphysical facts are;
we don't know if our sniper is domestic or foreign terror,
what color the chip on his shoulder is
or what we will do if the sniper chooses us tomorrow.

But when we go out now, we feel our nakedness.
Each step has a slender string attached.
And when we move, we move more quietly,
as we slide between the sinners and the snipers

and the summer,
in the simmering medicinal rain.

Nature

I miss the friendship with the pine tree and the birds
that I had when I was ten.
And it has been forever since I pushed my head
under the wild silk skirt of the waterfall.

What I had with them was tender and private.
The lake was practically my girlfriend.
I carried her picture in my front shirt pocket.
Even in my sleep, I heard the sound of water.

The big rock on the shore was the skull of a dead king
whose name we could almost remember.
Under the rooty bank you could dimly see
the bunk beds of the turtles.

Maybe twice had I said a girl's name to myself.
I had not yet had my weird first dream of money.

Nobody I know mentions these things anymore.
It's as if their memories have been seized, erased, and relocated
among flowcharts and complex dinner-party calendars.

Now I want to turn and run back the other way,
barefoot into the underbrush,
getting raked by thorns, being slapped in the face by branches.

Down to the muddy bed of the little stream
where my cupped hands make a house, and

I tilt up the roof
to look at the face of the frog.

III.

Requests for Toy Piano

Play the one about the family of the ducks
where the ducks go down to the river
and one of them thinks the water will be cold
but then they jump in anyway
and like it and splash around.

No, I must play the one
about the nervous man from Palestine in row 14
with a brown bag in his lap
in which a gun is hidden in a sandwich.

Play the one about the handsome man and woman
standing on the steps of her apartment
and how the darkness and her perfume and the beating of their hearts
conjoin to make them feel
like leaping from the edge of chance—

No, I should play the one about
the hard rectangle of the credit card
hidden in the man's back pocket
and how the woman spent an hour
plucking out her brows, and how her perfume
was made from the destruction of a hundred flowers.

Then play the one about the flower industry
in which the migrant workers curse their own infected hands,
torn from tossing sheaves of roses and carnations
into the back of the refrigerated trucks.

No, I must play the one about the single yellow daffodil
standing on my kitchen table
whose cut stem draws the water upwards
so the plant is flushed with the conviction

that the water has been sent
to find and raise it up
from somewhere so deep inside the earth
not even flowers can remember.

Barton Springs

Oh life, how I loved your cold spring mornings
of putting my stuff in the green gym bag
and crossing wet grass to the southeast gate
to push my crumpled dollar through the slot.

When I get my allotted case of cancer,
let me swim ten more times at Barton Springs,
in the outdoor pool at 6 A.M., in the cold water
with the geezers and the jocks.

With my head bald from radiation
and my chemotherapeutic weight loss
I will be sleek as a cheetah
—and I will not complain about life's

pedestrian hypocrisies;
I will not consider death a contractual violation.
Let my cancer be the slow-growing kind
so I will have all the time I need

to backstroke over the rocks and little fishes,
looking upwards through my bronze-tinted goggles
into the vaults and rafters of the oaks,
as the crows exchange their morning gossip

in the pale mutations of early light.
It was worth death to see you through these optic nerves,
to feel breeze through the fur on my arms,
to be chilled and stirred in your mortal martini.

In documents elsewhere I have already recorded
my complaints in some painstaking detail.
Now, because all things near water are joyful,
there might be time to catch up on praise.

Wild

In late August when the streams dry up
and the high meadows turn parched and blond,

bears are squeezed out of the mountains
down into the valley of condos and housing developments.

All residents are therefore prohibited
from putting their garbage out early.

The penalty for disobedience will be
bears: large black furry fellows

drinking from your sprinkler system,
rolling your trashcans down your lawn,

bashing though the screen door of the back porch to get their
first real taste of a spaghetti dinner,

while the family hides in the garage
and the wife dials 1-800-BEARS on her cell phone,

a number she just made up
in a burst of creative hysteria.

Isn't that the way it goes?
Wildness enters your life and asks

that you invent a way to meet it,
and you run in the opposite direction

as the bears saunter down Main Street
sending station wagons crashing into fire hydrants,

getting the police department to phone
for tranquilizer guns,

the dart going by accident into the
neck of the unpopular police chief,

who is carried into early retirement
in an ambulance crowned with flashing red lights,

as the bears inherit the earth,
full of water and humans and garbage,

which looks to them like paradise.

Disaster Movie

You were a jumbo jet, America,
      gone down in the jungle in my dream.

It must have been Borneo, or someplace tropical like that,
because vines had strangled the propellers into stillness,
rust was already licking the battered silver wings—

monkeys had commandeered the cockpit
and were getting drunk
      on the miniature bottles of vodka and Jack Daniels,

wearing the orange safety vests backwards
and spinning in the empty swivel chairs.

In the first-class cabin, the first-class passengers
had finished the last of the Chicken Kiev
        and were barricaded in,

while outside the economy fliers had gathered by the defunct fuselage
to take a vote
on whether to wait for rescue or to try to rescue themselves.

I couldn't believe that my twisted subconscious
would wreck a whole nation to make a point;
that my disgust with cell phones and beauty pageants would drive me to

ram it headfirst into the side of a hill,—its wings snapped off,
its captain decapitated,

its dependence on foreign oil
brought to a sudden conclusion.

And sure I knew that this apocalypse was a thin disguise
for my pitiful fear of being no good at ordinary life.

But what was sweet in the dream was the quiet
resilience of those little people:

someone using duct tape to make beds out of flotation cushions;
the stewardess limping past on crutches, as night seeped in.

The huge cracked tube of the plane
laid out on the floor like a broken toy.

An AA meeting in progress by one of the enormous, flattened tires.
And a woman singing in the dusk,
as she tended a fire
fed with an endless supply
            of safety manuals and self-help books.

Field Guide

Once, in the cool blue middle of a lake,
up to my neck in that most precious element of all,

I found a pale-gray, curled-upwards pigeon feather
floating on the tension of the water

at the very instant when a dragonfly,
like a blue-green iridescent bobby pin,

hovered over it, then lit, and rested.
That's all.

I mention this in the same way
that I fold the corner of a page

in certain library books,
so that the next reader will know

where to look for the good parts.

The Allegory of the Temp Agency

In the painting titled *The Allegory of the Temp Agency*,
the employers are depicted as wolves

with blood-red mouths and yellow greedy eyes,
pursuing the small-business employees through the dark forest
of capitalism. It is night and

by the light of the minimum-wage moon we can see
the long pink tongues of the bosses hanging out
and the dilated white eyeballs of the employees as they flee

through woods, lacking any sense of
solidarity or collective organizing power.

Upon closer inspection the leaves beneath their feet
are shredded dollar bills, which bear the distressed expressions
of ex-presidents, and the wind in the trees is making a long

howl of no health insurance or job security,
and no, it is not really a very good painting,
heavy handed in concept, and comic unintentionally in a way that

invites us to laugh at the desire for justice.
Rather, the painting shows that the artist was untalented,
and is an allegory of how difficult it is

to be both skillful and sincere,
which in turn explains why the art
that hangs in the lobbies of banks

and in the boardrooms of corporate office buildings
is often made of black-and-white slashes
against a background of melted orange crayon

or glowing lavender rectangles floating in gray haze,
works in which no human figures appear,
in which the Haves

do not appear to be chatting and laughing
as they eat their sushi
carved from the lives of the Have-Nots.

Jazz

I was driving home that afternoon
in some dilated condition of sensitivity
of the kind known only to certain poets
and more or less everybody else:

the sun of 6 P.M. glaring orangely through the trees
as through the bars of some kind of cage
and the poor citizens of Pecore Street waiting for the bus
with their sorrowful posture and bad feet—

I admit when I'm in one of these moods I find it
a little too easy to believe the trees are suffering,
to see the twisted branches as outstretched arthritic hands,
and the Spanish moss dripping from their scabby limbs
as parasitic bunting.

Someone had given me a jazz CD
he had thought I would enjoy,
but the song unfurling on the stereo that day
seemed a kind of torture-music,

played by wildly unhappy musicians
on instruments that had been bent in shipping,
then harnessed by some masochist composer
for an experiment on the nature of obstruction.

But of all the shrieking horns and drums
it was the passionate effort of a certain defective trumpet
to escape from its predetermined plot
that seemed to be telling a story that I knew:

veering back and forth, banging off the walls,
dripping a trail of blood
until finally it shattered through a window and disappeared.

For some reason I didn't understand,
it had to suffer before it was allowed to rest.
It was permitted to rest before being recaptured.

That was part of the composition.
That was the only kind of freedom
we were ever going to know.

The Perfect Moment

In the kisslike early summer twilight
under the weathered backboard

with the ragged net hanging from the hoop
and the ball going through it

as a long sweeping motion of the wind
bends all the marsh grass down at once

but only for a moment
before it springs back up

and Kath comes out of the house
with the iced tea and the newspaper

folded to the page of movie times,
I am thinking that if this

really is a perfect moment
it is probably up to the person

with stage-four lymphoma to say so
—but he is concentrating, setting up a corner shot,

trying to get his backspin right.

Sentimental Education

And when we were eight, or nine,
our father took us back into the Alabama woods,
found a rotten log, and with his hunting knife

pried off a slab of bark
to show the hundred kinds of bugs and grubs
that we would have to eat in time of war.

"The ones who will survive," he told us,
looking at us hard,
"are the ones who are willing do anything."
Then he popped one of those pale slugs
into his mouth and started chewing.

And that was Lesson Number 4
in *The Green Beret Book of Childrearing*.

I looked at my pale, scrawny, knock-kneed, bug-eyed brother,
who was identical to me,
and saw that, in a world that ate the weak,
we didn't have a prayer,

and next thing I remember, I'm working for a living
at a boring job
that I'm afraid of losing,

with a wife whose lack of love for me
is like a lack of oxygen,
and this dead thing in my chest
that used to be my heart.

Oh, if he were alive, I would tell him, "Dad,
you were right! I ate a lot of stuff
far worse than bugs."

And I was eaten, I was eaten,
I was picked up
and chewed
and swallowed

down into the belly of the world.

Demolition

They hang a big tube from the side of an office building
and through this esophagus the size
                              of an elevator shaft

they throw down furniture and
wire, chunks of plaster, ceiling tile and glass,
shag carpet, track lighting,

swivel chairs and lathe
crash and bashing into giant bins five floors below,
boing and banging down and this goes on for seven days.

I may be a grown man but that doesn't mean
I don't enjoy
the ingenuities of violence against matter,

which means I stand across the street with all the others guys
—wheelchair vet and hot-dog vendor,
junior attorney and the retiree—
in a little cluster of hypnotized testosterone.

I too am made of joists and stanchions,
of plasterboard and temperamental steel,
mortgage payments and severed index fingers,
ex-girlfriends and secret Kool-Aid-flavored dawns.

We gaze at the destruction and linger
the way a woman might stare awhile
at a too-expensive dress
in a big store window,

the way that moonlight looks at
an island in the middle of the sea—

island unnamed, and unashamed,
touched by the tide.

Not Renouncing

I always thought that I was going to catch Elena
in the library one afternoon, and she would shove me gently backwards
into the corridor of 822.7 in the Dewey Decimal System,
where we would do it in the cul-de-sac of 18th century drama.

Or I thought that we would meet by chance
in a bed and breakfast on the Delaware seashore,
and B and B each other in a helter skelter
of goose-down duvets and chamomile tea.

When I flew over the high plains of Wyoming,
I dreamed of taking off her cowboy shirt
and seeing her pale skin in a field of windswept prairie grass
that kept us completely out of sight,

and even in the British National Museum
I fell into a trance before the model
of the castle and the moat, the drawbridge
and the catapult, with all those moveable, moving parts.

This is the imagination of a man.
It wanes and waxes all through his life,
like a kind of tumescence. I am not bragging
and I'm not renouncing.

I stood in one garden,
looking over the fence at another.
I thought I had to change my life or give up,
but I didn't. Year after year

they kept growing into each other:
the dreamed into the real,
the real into the dreamed—the two gardens

sending their flexible, sinuous vines,
their tendrils and unbuttoning blossoms,
ceaselessly over their borders.

Powers

There is something clean and complete about autumn.
The ground looks swept under the trees.
The light has the quality of a mild detergent.
And the mailman walks down the street whistling,
sorting the Bills from the Janes.

Now the convulsions of feeling are over.
Summer has yielded its powers in exchange for peace.
The sun sets like an old commodities trader.
The artist begins to study the art of subtraction.

Turns out the real reason for growing up
was to learn what to do with suffering.
Not being surprised was the answer.
What else do you want to know?

In the grass, energy and matter continue their conversation.
Clouds drift along the horizon.
From somewhere a bulletin arrives:
terrible things in the distance.

But Sweetheart, haven't we had our servings of love?
Our thrilling moments of truth-in-speech?
What are we but monkeys who learned to drive cars,
who have the freedom to read or not to read
Proust?

On the marquee this week, I see
the movie about superheroes is here:
Flame Girl, who throws fireballs at crime.
Elastic Man, who stretches like a rubber band.
Kid Rock with the bulletproof skin.

Our powers are slightly different from theirs, it's true:
but you have the ability never to seem in a hurry
and mine, mine
is the simple, unrated power
to keep both of us amused.

Snowglobe

In an alleyway beside a nightclub
a miniature figure is vomiting:

that's how you know this is no
ordinary snowglobe. There are stockbrokers visible

in tall office buildings
staring at lit computer screens

for the slippery secret of money. It is late;
the babysitter turns up the volume on her headphones

to Mach 5
while the kids go out on the balcony to play.

Oh life! Are you even sober?
Can you touch your index finger

with the tip of your nose?
While great corporations drag their shades
                         across the land

like giant cloud formations,
sucking up pesos in one place,

raining down yuan in another.

Chopsticks and cancer and yellow cabs.
The interstate buzzing with metallic bees.

The greasy haze on the city shoulders.
While in the park a flock of poodles
escapes from the dogwalker's grip

like a pack of balloons.

At the bottom, a thickness that gathers,
like leftover gravy;

at the top, hope, like a pocket of air.
But what would happen if right now

it all turned upside down?

Muchness

I saw you in the rainy morning
from the window of the hotel room,
running down the gangplank to board the boat.
You were wearing your famous orange pants,

which are really apricot,
and the boat rocked a little
as you stepped on its edge.

You were going to work
with your backpack and sketchbook
and your bushy gray hair
which bursts out in weather
like a steel-wool bouquet.

That's how my heart is, I thought—
it lies coiled up inside of me, asleep,
then springs out and shocks me
with all of its muchness.

But as I was dreaming, your boat pulled away.
Then there was just the gray sheen
of the harbor left behind, like unpolished steel,

and the steep green woods that grow down to the shore
and the gauze of mist on the hills.

It was your vanished boat
that gave the scene a shape,
with its suggestion of journey and destination.

And the narrative then, having done its work,
it vanished too,
leaving just its affectionate cousin description behind.

—Description,
which lingers,
and loves for no reason.

Voyage

I feel as if we opened a book about great ocean voyages
and found ourselves on a great ocean voyage:
sailing through December, around the horn of Christmas
and into the January Sea, and sailing on and on

in a novel without a moral but one in which
all the characters who died in the middle chapters
make the sunsets near the book's end more beautiful.

—And someone is spreading a map upon a table,
and someone is hanging a lantern from the stern,
and someone else says, "I'm only sorry
that I forgot my blue parka; it's turning cold."

Sunset like a burning wagon train.
Sunrise like a dish of cantaloupe.
Clouds like two armies clashing in the sky.
Icebergs and tropical storms.
That's the kind of thing that happens on our ocean voyage—

And in one of the chapters I was blinded by love
and in another, anger made us sick like swallowed glass
and I lay in my bunk and slept for so long,

I forgot about the ocean,
which all the while was going by, right there, outside my cabin window.

And the sides of the ship were green as money,
        and the water made a sound like memory when we sailed.

Then it was summer. Under the constellation of the swan,
under the constellation of the horse.

At night we consoled ourselves
by discussing the meaning of homesickness.
But there was no home to go home to.
There was no getting around the ocean.
We had to go on finding out the story
                              by pushing into it—

The sea was no longer a metaphor.
The book was no longer a book.
That was the plot.
That was our marvelous punishment.

ACKNOWLEDGMENTS

Grateful acknowledgment is made to the editors of the following publications where many of these poems first appeared: *Alaska Quarterly Review* ('The Loneliest Job in The World'), *American Poetry Review* ('I Have News for You', 'Love', 'Poor Britney Spears', 'Hinge', 'In Praise of Their Divorce', 'Visitation', 'Description', 'Summer', 'Requests for Toy Piano', 'Nature', 'Hostess', 'The Situation', 'Wild', 'Expensive Hotel', 'Not Renouncing' and 'Nature'), *The American Scholar* ('Snowglobe'), *The Believer* ('Hard Rain'), *Café Review* ('Sentimental Education'), *Callaloo* ('The Story of White People'), *Florida Review* ('The Perfect Moment'), *Gulf Coast* ('Dialectical Materialism'), *Massachusetts Review* ('Foghorn'), *Provincetown Arts* ('Field Guide'), Ploughshares ('Jason the Real' and 'Powers'), *Poetry* ('Big Grab', 'At the Galleria', 'Barton Springs', 'Hostess', 'Cement Truck', 'Muchness' and 'Personal'), Pool ('Disaster Movie'), *Slate* ('The Story of the Father' and 'Confinement'), *Southern Review* ('Address to the Beloved'), *Speakeasy* ('Romantic Moment'), *Threepenny Review* ('Complicit with Everything'), *Tikkun* ('Demolition'), and *TriQuarterly* ('Jazz', 'Plastic', 'Food Court', 'Rhythm and Blues', 'Voyage' and 'The Allegory of the Temp Agency').

Some of these poems first appeared in the chapbooks *Hard Rain* (2005) and *Little Oceans* (2009). Many thanks to Ian Wilson, editor of Hollyridge Press.

'Jason the Real' is for Jason Shinder. 'Muchness' is for Kathleen Lee. 'Foghorn' is for Terrance Hayes. 'Dialectical Materialism' is for Campbell McGrath. 'Jazz' is for Barry Rackner.

I owe deep thanks to friends who have generously helped me with their scrupulous readership at different moments with this manuscript: Jason Shinder, Peter Harris, Ken Hart, Jennifer Grotz, Carl Dennis, B.J. Ward, and most especially, Kathleen Lee. And to members of my Houston writing group: Jennifer Grotz, Rich Levy, and Laurie Lambeth Clements.

I am grateful to the University of Houston for its support of writers. And I feel great thanks to the Jackson family for the Jackson Poetry Prize, to the Poetry Foundation for the Mark Twain Award, and to the family of O.B. Hardison for the award that bears his name. Thanks too to the Yaddo Corporation and the MacDowell Colony for the time and space they generously provided.